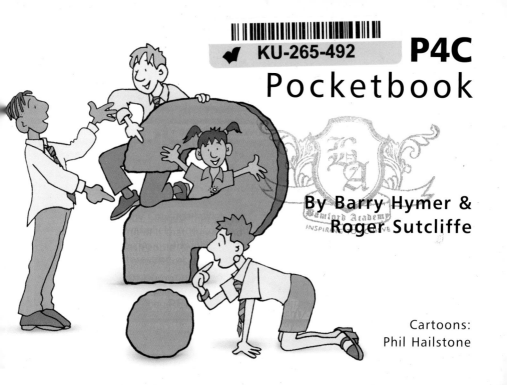

KU-265-492

P4C
Pocketbook

By Barry Hymer &
Roger Sutcliffe

Cartoons:
Phil Hailstone

Published by:

Teachers' Pocketbooks
Laurel House, Station Approach,
Alresford, Hampshire SO24 9JH, UK
Tel: +44 (0)1962 735573
Fax: +44 (0)1962 733637
Email: sales@teacherspocketbooks.co.uk
Website: www.teacherspocketbooks.co.uk

*Teachers' Pocketbooks is an imprint of
Management Pocketbooks Ltd.*

With thanks to Brin Best for his help in
launching the series.

All rights reserved. No part of this publication
may be reproduced, stored in a retrieval
system or transmitted in any form, or by any
means, electronic, mechanical, photocopying,
recording or otherwise, without the prior
permission of the publishers.

© Barry Hymer & Roger Sutcliffe 2012

This edition published 2012
ISBN: 978 1 906610 41 8

E-book ISBN: 978 1 908284 87 7

British Library Cataloguing-in-Publication
Data – A catalogue record for this book is
available from the British Library.

Design, typesetting and graphics by efex Ltd.
Printed in UK.

Contents

This Pocketbook is dedicated to the memory of Professor Matthew Lipman

'The approach that I have created in Philosophy for Children is about process, not content. It is not about prescribing any one philosophy to children but about encouraging them to develop their own philosophy, their own way of thinking about the world. It is about giving the youngest of minds the opportunity to express ideas with confidence and in an environment where they feel safe to do so.'

Matthew Lipman
(1923-2010)

Foreword

> *'Man seeks not happiness, but intensity.'* **Wittgenstein**
> *'So does Woman.'* **Man**

We'd like to think that you've bought this introduction to P4C because you sense it might accord with your values as an educator and with your beliefs about your pupils' potential for taking control of their own learning and lives. Perhaps three related reasons apply too:

1. You're interested in the questions your *pupils* might want to try to answer.
2. You've heard that P4C is a lot of fun – for you and for them.
3. You've heard that it *works*.

We hope that this book will provide evidence in support of all the above: P4C is indeed a learner-centred approach which uses pupils' own questions and desire to make sense of things as the 'core curriculum'. It's a process suffused with intense challenge for you and for them, and at the same time it's more fun than a basketful of kittens. And yes, it works – at so many levels.

Foreword

In what sense might P4C work for you? One extensive review of studies of P4C in several countries and in all phases of education concluded simply that '... *children can gain significantly both academically and socially*.' The authors of this review* also conducted a study of their own in 18 Scottish primary schools. This study provided evidence that one hour of philosophical enquiry each week can be highly cost-effective in promoting:

1. Development in cognitive ability.
2. Development in critical reasoning skills and dialogue in the classroom.
3. Emotional and social development.

It is the job of this Pocketbook to outline how you might secure these rewards for your own pupils. If we do our job well, we will make clear to you that P4C is far more than a friendly chat or even a guided discussion with your class – it involves supporting your pupils in creative connection-making, rigorously analysing concepts, and making sense of their world. With the tools you'll need and which we aim to provide, you will then go on to put these practices to good use in the classroom.

*Topping & Trickey, 2003

What is P4C?

 Choosing a Stimulus

 Any Questions?

 The Socratic Method

 Facilitating a P4C Enquiry

 Review

 Resources

What is P4C?

Deep roots

P4C is a modern approach with roots in the philosophy of ancient Greece – especially the dialogues of Socrates.

Matthew Lipman conceived P4C in the late '60s, a time of political and social turbulence. He sensed that it was time to restore the ancient values of philosophy – the critical pursuit of wisdom – to education for all young people, not just an intellectual elite. He was pragmatic in his approach to this task, beginning by writing 'philosophical' stories for children. These were used to engage children in philosophy's ongoing adventure of ideas.

Socrates did much the same in his marketplace dialogues with people from all walks of life (see pages 68-9 for an example).

Aims of P4C

> *'The aim of a thinking skills program such as P4C is to help children become more thoughtful, more reflective, more considerate and more reasonable individuals.'*
> **Professor Matthew Lipman**

In the '70s and '80s Lipman created a teacher education programme which has formed the basis for further development in about 60 countries.

In the UK, the 1990 BBC film *Socrates for 6 year-olds* helped stimulate interest. P4C is now practised with pupils of all ages – from the early years through to adulthood. You can do it with yours! With careful facilitation, high expectations, and over time, your pupils can learn to be *reasonable* – ie able to reason and willing to be reasoned with.

The 10-step process

A typical one-hour P4C session consists of roughly ten steps, each of which can be shaped to suit the ages or needs of the group (see pages 21-112):

1	**Getting set**	an activity that builds either community or enquiry skills.
2	**Presentation**	of a stimulus to please, puzzle or provoke.
3	**Thinking time**	private reflection leading to small group dialogue.
4	**Question-making**	focusing common interests into an inviting question.
5	**Question-airing**	considering the thinking behind the questions.
6	**Question-choosing**	deciding which question to concentrate on.
7	**First words**	suggestions as to how to begin answering the question.
8	**Building**	collaborating to develop understanding of and through the question.
9	**Last words**	each person's resting point in regard to content of enquiry.
10	**Review**	reflection on community process, progress and continuing project.

An example of P4C in practice

With her Year 3 class seated in a circle, Gemma played a game of 'Chinese Whispers' with them. She then read them 'Willow's Whispers' by Lana Button – a picture book about a soft-spoken girl who struggles to find her own voice.

After 40 seconds of eyes-closed thinking time, she asked them to work with a partner – sharing their thoughts and coming up with one question that they'd like to ask. Each pair wrote their question on a tablet/slate, and then 'aired' their question to the rest of the class – reading the question and saying why they'd asked it. The class then voted for each question in turn. Everyone could vote for as many questions as they wished...

An example of P4C in practice

...The question that attracted the most interest (16 votes) was, 'Why can't Willow speak loudly?'. Gemma asked the children to share their 'first responses' to this question with their partner, before leading a whole-class enquiry.

After a flurry of many possible explanations for Willow's soft voice, a child suggested, 'Maybe she could speak loudly, but her friends and teachers heard softly'. The enquiry then shifted to explorations of how we use our senses, and of appearance and reality.

The enquiry concluded with 30 seconds' quiet reflection and a 'last words' round, where the children could offer a short final response to the question, perhaps building on ideas they'd heard from others. Or they could comment on how well they thought they'd done in that P4C session – with ideas for doing even better next time.

Core concepts

> '... when you are a Bear of Very Little Brain, and Think of Things, you find sometimes that a Thing which seemed very Thingish inside you is quite different when it gets out into the open and has other people looking at it.'
> **A.A. Milne – House at Pooh Corner**

As you can see from Gemma's implementation of the usual ten-step process, P4C is refreshingly unique as a classroom activity in that there is no 'content' to stuff into your pupils' heads. Concepts themselves are the focus of investigation. They are the elemental building blocks by which we categorise and mentally construct the world we live in. We therefore regard P4C as a helpful way of exploring key concepts, not as a set syllabus or scheme of work. Not even Lipman's resources are seen as 'sacred texts'.

In introducing P4C to your pupils your task is to help them **construct conceptual maps** to navigate their increasingly complex world. Pooh's experience of finding that his understanding of words is different from others' is not uncommon. Most concepts are very personal. Think what the concept of *even* might mean to a mathematician as compared with a joiner or a football referee!

Responsive, responsible learners

'Conceptual map' is a fine term, but what is its classroom value? Our conceptual maps are not only the web of concepts that we build up over time, but also the many ways or patterns of thinking that steadily improve that web. In a world where there is any number of belief and value systems, there is a pressing need to help our pupils to develop robust concepts and ways of thinking of their own.

P4C sets about this task by explicitly valuing:

1. **Thinking skills** (such as questioning, reasoning, speculating and reflecting).
2. **Habits of mind** (such as inquisitiveness, reasonableness, courage, consideration of others).

In short, it cultivates responsive and responsible learners.

Philosophical teaching

As a teacher, you have a vital part to play in the process of nurturing and facilitating good thinking. No longer a slave to lesson/knowledge outcomes, you can design P4C sessions (ideally in collaboration with your pupils) to focus on skills, habits or concepts that need development.

Once an open/discussible question has been developed and chosen, and a concentrated enquiry is under way, you will model both wider ('floodlight') and deeper ('spotlight') thinking. You might initially use 'Socratic' questions (see pages 78-82) but will gradually develop your own techniques and art of facilitation. Having practised such facilitation, you may carry into your 'normal' teaching such philosophical qualities as:

- Breadth of mind – readiness to enquire beyond what you do know
- Intellectual humility – recognition that you don't know everything
- Respect for persons – appreciation that different people think in different ways
- Reasonableness – engagement in the process of good reasoning

Communities of enquiry

The P4C model of learning and teaching was influenced by the psychologist Lev Vygotsky (1896–1934) and the theory of social constructivism. But Lipman used an earlier phrase – *Community of Enquiry* – to label the process as he developed it. A community of enquiry can emerge in any subject where big concepts are identified and explored together.

Lipman's stories raised questions that can be located in traditional philosophical areas, eg:

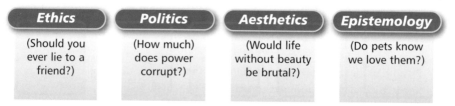

Ethics	**Politics**	**Aesthetics**	**Epistemology**
(Should you ever lie to a friend?)	(How much) does power corrupt?	(Would life without beauty be brutal?)	(Do pets know we love them?)

What makes such questions philosophical is the richness and contestability of their key concepts: *friend*, *power*, *beauty*, and *love* – which are by no means straightforward or commonly understood.

Basic conventions

Communities of enquiry are teams. These teams may work well from the start just by practising such basic conventions as:

- **OOPSAAT** – (Only One Person Speaks At A Time) – respecting others' rights
- **Be Open To Change Own Mind** – listening, ready to see things differently
- **Build On Previous Speakers** – linking with what others have said, and naming them
- **Give Evidence and Reasons** – giving and seeking reasons for what is said
- **Stay Calm and Friendly** – aiming to understand, not 'beat', others
- **Persist and Show Courage** – sticking to the point, and to your own beliefs
- **Appreciate That People Are Different** – sharing others' experiences and feelings
- **Keep A Sense Of Humour** – aiming for balance and positive outcomes

Encourage your class to frame ground rules of their own (see page 76), perhaps after the first session, or even before.

4C thinking – an holistic vision

Going beyond the basic conventions, communities of enquiry aim to make progress in **4C thinking** ie:

1. **C** aring (listening and valuing).

2. **C** ollaborative (speaking and supporting).

3. **C** reative (suggesting and connecting).

4. **C** ritical (questioning and reasoning).

Any of these could provide a 'skill' focus for a particular session, but the ideal is for your enquiry session to practise all 4Cs in balance – a bit like de Bono's Six Thinking Hats are designed to work together.

The expectation is that practice of skills translates into the development of **attitudes** or **dispositions**. For example, the caring thinker will be *respectful* and *appreciative* of others, the collaborative thinker will be *participative* and *constructive*, the creative thinker will be *independent* and *active*, and the critical thinker will be *reflective* and *reasonable*.

Research enquiry and reflection enquiry

Once the spirit of enquiry is well established in your class, it will alternate quite naturally between research enquiry (information-seeking) and reflection enquiry (insight-seeking).

Don't fret if your pupils' questions and responses seem overly concrete or 'empirical' at the beginning. The question Gemma's class chose (page 12) was hardly stellar! Remember we need both information (content) to pursue and critical reflection (careful analysis and synthesis) to interrogate the information for insights that are meaningful, true and useful.

When a child asks, *'How can a tree talk?'* you have a chance both to **enquire** (eg *'What do we mean by 'talk'?'*) and to **reflect** critically on the responses (eg *'So do only humans 'talk'?'*). You'll soon see that even apparently concrete and 'unphilosophical' questions can contain conceptual potential. The best way of establishing the spirit of enquiry is to practise philosophical enquiry deliberately, using the ten steps outlined on page 10.

P4C's place in the curriculum

Despite your best intentions, you may find the opportunity to practise P4C squeezed out of your timetable. To have the sort of success that was achieved in research studies, you need a minimum of one P4C session a week. You might manage this by turning the first literacy (or English) lesson of the week into a P4C session. Or you might build the P4C process into your RE or History programme. With some thought, it can be done – and is done – in Science and Maths too. But the most innovative and potentially most influential approach is to reconstruct PSHE, Citizenship and PLTS as PSP – Personal and Social Philosophy.

With its traditional emphasis on good thinking leading towards the good life, Philosophy is the obvious 'subject' into which to combine what are now treated as separate curriculum areas. But Philosophy is more than a subject: it is a true discipline, likely to improve thinking and learning across the curriculum.

The next five sections of this Pocketbook will help you to translate the theory of P4C into classroom practice, using the ten-step model outlined on page 10.

What is
P4C?

 Choosing a
Stimulus

 Any
Questions?

 The Socratic
Method

 Facilitating a
P4C Enquiry

 Review

 Resources

Choosing a
Stimulus

Getting set – seating

The ideal starting point for your class is for everyone to be seated in a circle, with desks pushed to one side. This breaks down hierarchies, creates an expectation of involvement, and allows everyone to see everyone else. Be careful of hidden messages though: make sure that you're at their level. If they're on the carpet, you should be too. If they're on standard-issue plastic chairs, it isn't a good idea for you to be on a crushed-velvet chaise longue!

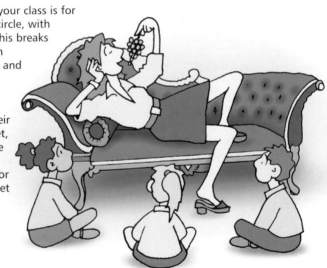

Getting set – stilling

To do justice to the forthcoming stimulus it's important to be receptive to it. In the Quaker phrase, your pupils should approach the stimulus *'with hearts and minds prepared'*. Stilling activities can play a useful role when the group needs calming at the start of a session. Try one of these:

 Kinaesthetic – Hold a minute's silence (tough at first, but like all learning, easier with practice; eyes shut and a focus on breathing can help).

 Auditory – Play an appropriate (slow, calm, relaxing) piece of music.

 Visual – Hold a minute's silent reflection on a 'visual magnet', eg a lava-lamp, a flickering candle, or an upturned sealed glass jar containing water and glitter (the glitter slowly descends).

 Emotional – Lead a guided visualisation: with their eyes closed, pupils are taken for an imaginative 'walk' – in the woods, on a beach, looking down from a hot-air balloon. In their minds, what do they see, hear, touch, smell, taste? Look for details, particulars, new and familiar imaginative sensations.

Getting set – games

As your pupils become more used to P4C, you might find that the need for a stilling activity reduces, and you can proceed to a more active game or even directly to the presentation of the stimulus. Short games foster a spirit of intellectual playfulness, risk-taking and attentiveness to other members of the group. Here are five P4C favourites:

1. **Changing places** *'Find a different chair to sit on if you think you can … '* (eg define a friend, say how humans are different from other animals, etc). This game has the added merit of separating best friends and generally stirring the social pot. Neighbours could be asked to share their ideas before each succeeding 'thinking challenge'. For further examples, see pages 123-124.
2. **Name 'n move** (another change places game). All stand up. You start by saying the name of someone whilst walking towards them. They must *immediately* vacate their chair (for you to sit on), say the name of *someone else* and sit on that person's chair, and so on.

Getting set – more games

3. **Yeah but, no but** Ask a partner a series of questions, trying to get him or her to say '*yes*' or '*no*'. Starting with five, they lose a life every time they say '*yes*' or '*no*' or pause too long before replying.

4. **OOPSAAT** – Only One Person **Sits** At A Time (compare with page 17). From a standing position, the group must sit down one at a time. If two or more start sitting down at the same time, all must stand up and try again. Rules – no words, no gestures, no patterns. **Tip** – slowly does it!

5. **Other life** If you could be someone else for a day… Nominate someone dead or alive, real or fictional, but give a reason for your choice. Invite others to support or doubt reasons.

I don't know!

What's the point of a stimulus?

A stimulus is intended to get your pupils thinking and asking questions from a shared experience. Slightly expanded, the following five-stage sequence can be identified:

Some stimuli pique more interest, evoke more thought, open more dialogue and raise more questions than others. How can we be sure to choose a good stimulus? In P4C little is certain, but in this section we will use the notion of *narrative plot* as a tool to assist in the selection or creation of good stimuli.

The nature of narrative (1)

E M Forster observed that *'The king died and then the queen died'* is a story, whereas *'The king died and then the queen died of a broken heart'* is a plot. A story consists of:

Event (what happened?)
Character (who are the agents?)
Time (when did this happen?)

What plot brings to the narrative is **causality**, a reason for or consequence of an event. Causality gives meaning to an event and allows us to construct multiple connections as this meaning is expanded. With causality, events become *interesting* to us. You can easily see, therefore, how a well-chosen extract from a novel, fairy-story or picture book might act as a stimulus for enquiry.

The following complete tale by Ernest Hemingway consists of only six words:

> For sale:
> baby shoes.
> Never worn.

Without any one narrative element being settled or explicit, all four are captured and so it sparks the sequence of interest, thought, dialogue and questioning that all good stimuli do.

The nature of narrative (2)

The *Da Vinci Code* author Dan Brown says: *'For me, the ideal topic has no clear right and wrong, no definite good and evil, and makes for great debate'*.

Replace 'topic' with 'stimulus' and you're onto a P4C winner: the ideal stimulus holds ethical, aesthetic and logical ambiguities and subtleties within its narrative and invites us to give these meaning. It chooses:

- Doubt over certainty
- Creativity over the commonplace
- The lived experience over the known fact
- The broadly conceptual over the narrowly particular

The nature of narrative (3)

Taking Hemingway's baby shoes tale, here are a few possible responses:

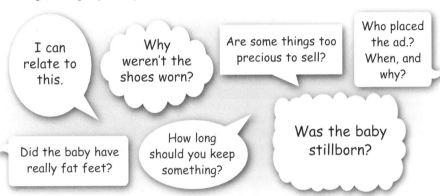

I can relate to this.

Why weren't the shoes worn?

Are some things too precious to sell?

Who placed the ad.? When, and why?

Did the baby have really fat feet?

How long should you keep something?

Was the baby stillborn?

But how does the narrative model (event, character, time, causality) apply to, say, an artefact or a piece of music or an obscure historical record? The next page offers a couple of examples.

Non-narrative narrative?

	KS2 – Tudors	KS4 – Holocaust
Stimulus	Reproduction of a carved wooden string mill toy.	*'SS Profitability Calculations on the Exploitation of Concentration Camp Inmates' (average life expectancy nine months, net profit RM 1631 + 'proceeds from utilisation of bones and ash'.)*
Event	What is this? How might it be used?	What are these calculations? What do they signify?
Character/s	Who might use (have used) this? Who might make (have made) this?	What kind of people might do these calculations? Were they forced to, or did they choose to? Could they exist today?
Time	When might it be (or have been) used?	What is the historical context for these calculations?
Causality	Why would it be made/used? For what purpose? Is it a tool, a toy, a piece of art? What makes something a toy/art? Could anything be a toy/art? When is a toy not a toy? Etc.	Does the context confer understanding or legitimacy? Does everyone have empathy? In certain contexts, does anyone?

Could anything be a stimulus (1)?

'*Philosophy begins when children start exploring the meanings of words.*' **Lipman**

Children experienced in P4C are able to attach the narrative model to the slightest of stimuli – a used bus ticket, a leaf, a game of rock-scissors-paper – even a single word! Take this line from Lipman's book *Kio & Gus*: '*Her real name is Augusta*'.

Few would argue that this disembodied line constitutes a story in itself, but an experienced P4C-er could interrogate the keywords ('*real*' or '*name*') and buttress these with *character* (Augusta herself, or the people who named her), *event* (her naming), *time* (when did they name her?) and *causality* (why does she have more than one name?).

Could anything be a stimulus (2)?

After completing the chart below,* pupils could move on to extension questions – eg: Why am I named differently? What's the purpose of a nickname? Does everything have a name? Do we name what we *do*? Do we name things that don't exist? Look in each instance for examples or counter-examples.

Name on my birth certificate	Name my parents use for me	Name my friends use for me	Name my teacher uses for me	Name my pet uses for me!

*Adapted from the Instructional Manual to accompany 'Kio & Gus'.

Could anything be a stimulus (3)?

Alternatively (or additionally), focusing on the word 'real', ask your pupils to consider these words, and perhaps to come up with some more. Place them in the Venn diagram, giving reasons:

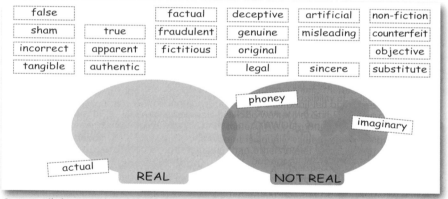

Once pupils have worked through these stimulus follow-up exercises, they could start generating questions (see Any Questions? chapter).

Squeezing philosophy from the stimulus

It might be tempting for you to see the 'point' of P4C as being contained in the group enquiry step (see 'Facilitating a P4C Enquiry' chapter). But every step has philosophical purpose – as the previous two pages show. The stimulus in each case was minimal, but we tried through the associated follow-up exercises to shed some light on the concepts *'name'* and *'real'*. What words surround the concepts? Are they synonyms, antonyms, related or unrelated? You're already familiar and skilled at the task of building your pupils' vocabulary but it's a tougher task to develop your pupils' skills of:

- Classification
- Definition
- Discrimination (by degree or kind)
- Discovering of alternatives and exceptions

In short, learning new words is an educationally worthy task for you and your pupils. But truly to understand the concepts that words rest on goes beyond that to the next level.

Concept Corners

A good occasional exercise for growing your pupils' 'conceptual muscles' goes by the name of *Concept Corners* or *Concept SPEC*.

If a stimulus leads to your children coming up with a rich concept that is worth spending some time exploring in its own right, it can be written in the middle of a rectangle. This is then divided into four equal quadrants headed respectively: **Synonyms**, **Phrases**, **Examples**, **Connections**. Each quadrant (or corner) then represents a different task, ie to think of:

1. **S**ynonyms (or antonyms) – words of similar or opposite meaning.
2. **P**hrases (or sentences) in which the concept is used in normal speech.
3. **E**xamples (or situations) where the concept can be seen to apply.
4. **C**onnections (or associations) – things or ideas the concept calls to mind.

Your pupils could undertake all four tasks individually, or collaboratively in small groups. Alternatively, you could divide the whole class into four and ask them to split into the four corners of the room, to work on just one task per group. Rich discussion and learning can ensue when ideas are then shared and compared as a whole class.

Example of Concept Corners

Synonyms (or antonyms)
Person/People
Humane/Kind/Inhuman(e)
Humanist
Anthropology
Animal/Beastly

Phrases (or sentences)
Human skeleton/remains
Human error
When was the first human?
Humans are different from animals
To err is human, to forgive divine

HUMAN

Connections (or associations)
Planet earth
Habitation/Cities
Language/Culture/Creativity
Tools/Technology
Flesh and bones/Biped/Brains

Examples (or situations)
Anyone reading this!
Babies/Children
Neanderthals?
Humans at war
Men on the moon

Groups could then prepare to answer:
'What do your items tell us about what it is to be human?'
At some point it might be interesting to use the items to try to construct a definition.

Suitable for more experienced groups

...of music (no lyrics) or preferably two contrasting pieces
...rately 'minimalist' stimulus (eg a jigsaw piece, a pen, a single word)

Suitable for developing groups

...oman's stories or other extracts from a (text-based) story or novel
...ought-provoking poems or song lyrics
...ames for thinking and drama (eg hot-seating)
...ialogues (eg from a play script, read by members of the group)
...n experience from real-life (eg the news, or personal experience)

Suitable for beginning groups

Thought-provoking picture-books, parables, pairs of proverbs
Short films, YouTube clips and video excerpts
Other visual stimuli (eg photos, artwork, posters)
Unusual artefacts and objects

Multiple hooks

Though we've tried to show that even minimal stimuli ⸱
don't recommend introducing P4C to a new group with ⸱
ticket. In the early months, choose something that carrie⸱
explicitly, offering the class multiple hooks and handles ⸱
and causality.

As a very rough-and-ready guide, on the next
page is a stimulus hierarchy based not on
the age of the participants, but on how
experienced they are in P4C. See this as a
rule of thumb only. So much depends on
your class's maturity, interests, concentration
skills, preparedness to think independently and
inter-dependently, etc.

- A piece
- A delib⸱

- L
- T
- C
- ⸱

Stimuli from the curriculum

P4C stimuli can certainly be based around an aspect of the set curriculum that you may wish to teach. P4C is less about teaching than creating a space for enquiry-led learning though, so be warned: the questions raised and the question voted for may bear no relation to your intended content-objective.

If time for enquiry is limited and there is a strong need to gear the time towards a particular curriculum concept (eg *sustainability* in geography), on the next page you'll find a few ways of preserving the spirit of open enquiry whilst also enabling some conceptual focus.

Curriculum-centred stimuli

1. Choose a stimulus that has such a concept 'embedded' in it and is fit for enquiry, ie one that stimulates insight-seeking (reflection) questions as much as information-seeking (research) questions. For instance, an aerial photograph of the tracks formed during a logging operation in a forest, the whole resembling the shape of a tree.

2. Begin the session with a short introduction to the curriculum concept, perhaps an explanation, or better still an activity of 'connections' (such as Concept Corners on page 35) – a gathering of words/ideas that might be associated with the concept in question. Still invite the pupils to create questions of their own from the stimulus, but then engage them in deciding which of the questions may be best related to the curriculum concept. Set aside those questions for closer attention later.

3. Use the next 15-20 minutes to 'air' the other questions, enabling them to explore one or more of them 'openly', without constraint. But finally return to the questions set aside, which should provide a good platform for enquiry into the curriculum concept.

Good stimuli – four elements

Whether you choose a curriculum-lite or a curriculum-focused stimulus, be sure that it incorporates some (or all) of these elements:

1. **Big ideas** – content rich in philosophically evergreen concepts such as truth, beauty, happiness or power.
2. **Contestable ideas** – content which encourages intellectual argument and exchange of contrasting views. Ethical dilemmas and tough choices are rich terrain here.
3. **Surprising ideas** – content which jars, intrigues and surprises. Much modern art uses this device, eg juxtaposing images of innocence and violence, or modifying a Mercedes Benz logo to resemble a Nazi death's head symbol.
4. **Connectable ideas** – characters and plot-lines that elicit empathy and identification.

Using picture books (F/KS1 – ages 3-7)

In the UK, Karin Murris was the first to grasp the potential of good picture books as stimuli for philosophical enquiry. They have proved their worth over time and are particularly useful as stimuli for groups of all ages in the early steps of their P4C development. Below are three examples and you'll find lists of several others on pages 120-122

Book	▶	***Not a Stick*** by Antoinette Portis (see also its predecessor, ***Not a Box***)
Summary	▶	A little pig finds a broken branch and uses it imaginatively in a variety of make-believe scenarios, repeatedly contradicting an invisible admonisher ('*Watch where you point that stick*', etc) with the words, '*It's not a stick!*'
Dominant theme/s	▶	Alternative imaginative uses for an everyday object; seeing things from a child's eye view
Questions to elicit and explore key concepts	▶	• *What is a stick?* • *When does a branch (or even a tree) become a stick?* • *Is a telegraph pole (or a match) a stick?* • *Can a stick also be 'not-a-stick'?* • *Why can't the 'voice' see what the pig sees?* • *Why doesn't the pig see what the 'voice' sees?*

Using picture books (KS2 – ages 7-11)

Book	▶ *The Wretched Stone* by Chris Van Allsburg
Summary	▶ Written in the form of log excerpts from the captain of a tall-ship. A resourceful and accomplished crew discover a strange rock on an uncharted and sinister island. They take it on board the ship, and as the days pass the rock exerts a magnetic hold on the crew, whose behaviour and nature take a worrying turn … As with many books by this author, brilliantly and enigmatically told and illustrated.
Dominant theme/s	▶ The creeping impact of electronic media on our minds and behaviour
Questions to elicit and explore key concepts	▶ • *Is the captain a good leader? What makes a good leader?* • *How might a crew member's account of the journey differ from that of the captain? Is any one account a true account?* • *What does the rock represent? Do we have rocks like these in our own lives?* • *What influences our behaviour? If our behaviour changes, are we changed?* • *If we've changed in some way, can we ever change back?*

Using picture books (KS3/4 – ages 11-16)

Book	▶ ***The Island*** by Armin Greder
Summary	▶ A man is washed up on a small island. The inhabitants accept him reluctantly and treat him harshly. Their suspicions and resentments feed off each other and ultimately lead to the man being forced back to sea. They build great barriers to future 'invasions'.
Dominant theme/s	▶ Immigration, the 'othering' of minorities, justification of inhumane acts
Questions to elicit and explore key concepts	▶ • *What is the story about? What key ideas are expressed?* • *Are we responsible for our own fate?* • *What makes us the same as/different from others?* • *What was the fisherman's motivation for helping the man? What are our motivations for helping others?* • *Can we 'get back to our business' knowing there is suffering in our world?* • *How do we justify our own prejudices?* • *What are the origins of fear?* • *Can we suppress our humanity?*

What is
P4C?

 Choosing a
Stimulus

 Any
Questions?

 The Socratic
Method

 Facilitating a
P4C Enquiry

 Review

 Resources

Any Questions?

The value of questions in general

> 'The test of a good teacher is not how many questions he can ask his pupils that they will answer readily, but how many questions he inspires them to ask which he finds it hard to answer.' **Alice Wellington Rollins, (1847 – 1897)**

You may agree with Indira Gandhi that 'The power to question is the basis of all human progress'. You may, like most thoughtful teachers, know that questions are where it's at! Yet the statistics of how many questions teachers ask compared to how many children ask on average per day – a ratio of around 400:1 – aren't flattering.

Moreover, in recent studies, only 8% of primary teachers' questions demanded higher-order thinking (reflection and reasoning) – and only 4% of secondary teachers'. This isn't because you doubt the value of your pupils' own questions, but because a test-and-content-centred education system seems to leave few gaps for our pupils' curiosity. It's easier to use questions as a tool for checking the efficiency of our transmission: if they give us the right answer, we've done our job; if they don't, we haven't.

Question fluency – from Kipling to Kagan

How can we sustain and develop the curiosity that is so evident in young children?

We can help them practise using the tools of formal enquiry, perhaps building on Kipling's rhyme: *I keep six honest serving men, They taught me all I knew. Their names are What and Why and When, And How and Where and Who*. Or by using Spencer Kagan's Question Matrix, for example to interrogate a picture:

	Is / Was?	Does / Did?	Can / Could?	Would?	Will?	Might?
Who						
What						
Where						
When						
How						
Why						

Pupils could be asked to create six questions, beginning with each one of Kipling's 'serving men', followed by any one of the 'auxiliaries'. Use of different auxiliaries could be explored. More varied questions can start simply with the auxiliaries.

Question fluency – games and activities

Here are a few more ways of encouraging your pupils to ask questions:

What's my story? – present an object to pupils, and ask them to imagine it could answer their questions. How many questions can they create in pairs – and how good are they?

What's my question? – announce that 'X' (eg *a brick*, or *five*) is 'the answer', and see how many different questions can be created that have that same answer.

Question chains – start with any question that has come up recently, eg '*Which animals have spots?*' Then invite new questions to be made, perhaps written down, that contain one word from the original, eg 'How many different *animals* are there in the world?', 'How many *worlds* are there?', etc.

Tag questions – using text on paper or on screen, show how many statements can be questioned just by tagging them with '*is/n't it?*' or '*do/n't they?*', etc. Texts that contain several *claims* are the best (*aren't they?*) – especially news articles.

From thinking time to question-making

In a full P4C session the aim is to build on your pupils' basic question-making skills so that over time they become expert questioners. Thinking Time is an important part of this building, reducing the chance that a rich stimulus might be met with poor questioning. Here are some things to try:

*   Remind the pupils in advance of the stimulus to look/listen **thoughtfully**, so that when they have quiet time afterwards they have something to think about

*   Again in advance, put them into **wondering** mode, eg *'let your minds wonder (or even wander!)'* or suggest the sentence stem, *'I wonder …'*

*   After the stimulus, suggest that they think of anything in it that they found **'puzzling, pleasing or provoking'** or **'intriguing, interesting or irritating'**

*   Ask them to think of two or three **'talking points'** or **'points to ponder'** or **'big ideas'** (see page 51)

What if early questioning is lower-order?

Developing higher-order questioning skills has benefits beyond just your P4C sessions. A review of 37 studies suggested that increasing the proportion of higher-order questions (HOQ) to 50% significantly improved pupil attitude and performance. If your pupils' questioning seems not to be developing much beyond the 'closed' or concrete, they may need to be given extra time, before or after enquiry sessions, to think about questions.

One way to improve their HOQ is to encourage HOT (Higher Order Thinking), especially **analysis** and **evaluation** of lists of questions. Questions may be classified in various ways: by subject, by difficulty (to answer), by importance, by interest, etc.

Sample exercise for younger children:

> Collect examples of your pupils' questions from past stimuli and randomly assign one to each pair. Each pair must decide if the question is a) easy to answer, b) hard to answer, c) somewhere in between. In turn, each pair reads their question, announces their decision and justifies their answer. Peers are encouraged to challenge each decision, with reasons. Each question is finally placed in one of three 'sorting hats'.

What if early questioning is lower-order?

Older pupils might be encouraged to classify questions using traditional philosophical terms: ethics, politics, aesthetics and epistemology. Simpler versions of these might be: (questions about) right and wrong, rights and responsibilities, what we like and value, knowledge and reality – including questions about experience.

Another way of developing a sense of the philosophical is to focus on big ideas (or 'rich' or 'juicy' concepts). Most people have an intuitive sense that 'power' is a bigger/richer idea than 'peanuts'. Your class might begin to fill in an A to Z chart of such ideas or concepts, drawing them from across the curriculum, not only from P4C enquiries.

Analysis of such ideas might be helped by reference to 'the 3Cs':

- **Common** (to people/cultures across the world)
- **Central** (to the way people think about the world and their lives)
- **Contestable** (either in meaning or in value)

Try these criteria on: Animals, Bullies, Causes, Dreams, Education, Fun, Great, Holiday, Independence...

The Question Quadrant

Invented by an Australian teacher and popularised by Phil Cam, this tool (slightly adapted) has been successfully used to help pupils classify and create questions:

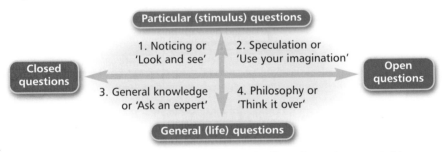

Particular (stimulus) questions

1. Noticing or 'Look and see'

2. Speculation or 'Use your imagination'

Closed questions

Open questions

3. General knowledge or 'Ask an expert'

4. Philosophy or 'Think it over'

General (life) questions

You could use The Question Quadrant to analyse the lists of questions created in your P4C sessions. As a stand-alone exercise, it might work best in response to a picture. If pupils have used the Question Matrix to interrogate a picture, a natural next step might be to put each of their questions into the appropriate quadrant. If a question seems to straddle two quadrants, discussion could help clarify the categories. If a quadrant is under-populated, extra questions could be created to fill it.

Moving questions up the levels

In our experience pupils tend not to ask as many 1st quadrant ('noticing') questions as teachers. On the other hand, they do respond with quite a lot of 2nd quadrant ('speculative') questions – especially trying to work out intentions/motivations. Many of their questions begin with *'Why …?'*.

Before or during an enquiry you might suggest that a question such as *'Where was she going?'* might be **generalised** into *'Where might she/you go? (And why?)'*. Or a question such as *'Why did he …?'* might become *'Why would someone … ?'*

A specific exercise could show how apparently simple 'factual' questions may 'grow' into bigger, more conceptual, questions. For example, *'Who looked after the children?'* → *'Who might have looked after them'?* → *'Who should have looked after them?'* → *'Can children look after themselves?'* → *'Is looking after different from keeping an eye on?'*

There are two common directions of growth. One is towards the more conceptual or **general** (*Always?*) and the other is towards the more **moral** (*Should?*).

Question-making

Your class should improve the quality and fluency of its question-making just through regular practice, say within 6–12 sessions, especially if time is spent thinking about questions outside of P4C sessions as well. But here are a couple of variations of the question-making step that might further speed up the learning:

Collaborative Creation (early communities) – groups are given a minute or two to decide what they most want to talk about. A spokesperson for each group in turn articulates this to the whole group. For each such 'talking point', either spontaneous suggestions for enquiry are elicited, or individuals or groups have another short amount of time to write down a possible question. The original group chooses which one they like best.

Question Fest (more experienced communities) – individuals write down as many questions as they can within two or three minutes. They then pair, share, and choose each other's 'best' question to put to the group. They could then go 'Twos into Fours' – each pair choosing one of the other pair's two questions to put forward. If they have time, they could discuss possible improvements to each other's questions.

Airing questions – thinking behind or ahead

The simplest way of airing questions is to ask each pair/group to say something about the 'thinking behind' their question – or 'how they came to their question'.

If one person speaks confidently for the group, you might just invite any others to add to or even qualify what that person said. You could also lead the way in **questioning the question**, eg by asking for *clarification*, or *elaboration*. This could include whether the question is intended to address an issue specifically in the context of the stimulus, or more generally.

A more advanced version of this process is to invite the questioners and/or others to say what concepts or further questions they think the question might lead on to. This is generally called 'thinking ahead', though it can also be labelled 'questions behind the question' or, perhaps more imaginatively, 'questions in waiting'.

Airing questions – linking and lumping

Once the questions have been created on paper (usually on a board or chart in early sessions, but perhaps on A4 slates once groups have got the hang of making questions), get your pupils to spend a little time reflecting on them before settling on one to start with.

A favourite approach is to see what **links**, if any, there are between questions. Two or more questions can be shown to link, sometimes being placed next to each other. Encourage the link to be made explicit. You're looking for more than *'They are both about X'*. Perhaps they could both be linked back to part of the stimulus. Or perhaps you might say, *'But what are they asking about X?'*

Once the nature of the link or similarity between questions is clear, a further challenge can be made by asking, *'And now, what is the difference between them?'*

Occasionally, if there is no significant difference, you could 'lump' questions together as one, especially to avoid splitting any vote. Finally, it's also fine to attempt to merge two rather different questions, but be ready to drop the attempt if it gets bogged down!

Airing questions – celebrating or circulating

Another favourite is to invite anyone to 'celebrate' each question in turn, eg beginning, '*I like X's question because …*'

Normally it is enough for only one person to do this per question, but if there is time you might ask if anyone else has a different reason for liking it. A small conversation could even be opened up by inviting comments on the reasons, but be careful not to let the conversation drift into what amounts to a full enquiry before all the other questions have been aired and a starter question decided upon.

A buzzy alternative is called 'circulating' or 'conversation carousel'. The group forms two concentric circles, standing up, the inner one facing outwards, the outer one facing inwards (everyone should thus be facing a 'talking partner'). Partners discuss one question for just one minute, before the facilitator calls 'time' and one or other circle rotates, so as to create different partners for the next question – and so on until all the questions have been aired. The same effect can be achieved more simply if two lines stand opposite each other and each person moves one place clockwise.

Question-choosing

For reasons of time it is usual for communities to want to focus on a single question for a full enquiry. That said, it's quite OK for you to split the time available between two or more questions if that's what your pupils wish to do. They could even be encouraged to make an 'agenda' or agreement to move from one to another – perhaps planning for the enquiry to run into a second session.

Univote   This is a conventional way of choosing a question to start an enquiry – explained as 'one vote per person'. With younger children this is often done as a 'blind' vote, perhaps with children facing outwards from the circle. They could also be asked to agree that no one should vote for their own question, but after discussing this, they/you may not feel it is necessary. This system can result in comparatively few votes per question, in which case it might be sensible to vote again between the three or four questions with the most votes.

Omnivote   This is a common and interesting alternative, in which people can vote for as many questions as they like – including their own, and even including all of them (hence, 'omni'). If two or three questions end up almost 'equal', then again a second round with just one or two votes per person might be advised.

Question-choosing

Multivote This is best thought of as any number of votes between one (uni) and all (omni). The simplest version, often used for very young children, is to allow two votes (which might or might not include their own). If three or more votes are allowed, this is often done by handing out counters, cards, matches or the like, to be placed on the questions.

3/2/1 This is a more challenging system whereby people choose their three favourite questions, and rank them in order of preference. As each question is read out, they hold up one hand (ie one vote) for their 3rd favourite, two hands (ie two votes) for their 2nd, and they stand up (three votes) for their 1st. It can be particularly helpful in this case for a volunteer to act as an independent 'teller', counting/confirming the tally.

Motorvote Pupils move to stand by/on the question they most like. If no question has a clear majority, anyone standing on the question with fewest votes is asked to transfer their vote to another question, perhaps justifying their choice. This process (**STV – Single Transferable Vote**) continues until one or two popular questions emerge. If two questions tie on votes, you can reduce 'hard' feelings by evenly sharing the time available for enquiry.

Valuing questions

However tempting it often is, don't try to influence the outcome of the vote! Run with the chosen question and squeeze what you can from it (see chapter on facilitating an enquiry for techniques to do this), remembering that P4C involves a process of gradual discernment and improvement – it's not about a polished product.

As pupils get better at creating and critiquing questions they tend to put more time into that process. It often seems a pity to set aside the results of their thinking to focus on just one question. You might wish therefore to do one or more of the following:

- **Leave** them on the board or floor for possible reference during the enquiry
- **Invite** further reflection on them during Last Words or in Review
- **Hang** them on a wall (or 'airing line') for reference in days or weeks to come
- **Lodge** them in a 'question box' for drawing one or more out later by lottery
- **Record** them in a (class or personal) 'philosophy log/book' or 'enquiry diary'
- **Copy** the question (their own or others') for taking home to discuss – 'home talk'

We shall also look, later in this book, at how to take questions back into the curriculum.

Enquiry question examples

Below and on the next page are some examples of enquiry questions generated from rich stimuli presented to a mixed-ability class of 36 Year 5 pupils. The class had been doing P4C since Year 4, so had developed some expertise in asking authentic, quadrant 4 questions.

Stimulus	Chosen Question/s
Jar of rocks, sand and pebbles	What are the rocks, sand and pebbles in your life?
What kind of Liar are You? Poem by Carl Sandburg	Do people have an inbuilt need to lie? Are people always true to themselves?
Bilbo Baggins: A Hobbit's Tale by JRR Tolkien	Is it worth losing a friend to win a war?
Images of war-affected places	Is war planned and why?
Quotation from the Indian philosopher Shantanand Sarawati and images of urban graffiti.	Do the rich see the poor as different from themselves?
Ballad of *Bedd Gelert*	Is it right to kill to protect someone or something?
Images of different places, objects and people	Do people value their outside more than their inside?

With thanks to Kelly Pope, St Lawrence CE Primary School, Gnossall, Staffordshire LA

More examples

Stimulus	Chosen Question/s
Name or person? From Lao Tsu (7th Century BC)	Would you prefer to win a game and lose a friend or lose a game but win a friend?
Images of city life	Why do people choose to be cruel?
The Big Big Sea by Martin Waddell	Does memory exist in the past or the present? What is the difference between a memory and a dream and is one more important than the other?
The Mousehole Cat by Antonia Barber and Nicola Bayley	Why is the storm-cat important and feared?
Extract from *Heaven Eyes* (p.77) by David Almond	Does the fact that we see something make it real?
I am, poem by Laura (Anti-Bullying Alliance)	Are bullies the actual victims?
Pupils' own dance work, based on *Remember* by Christina Rossetti	Does memory interfere with imagination? Can we control our destiny?

With thanks to Kelly Pope, St Lawrence CE Primary School, Gnossall, Staffordshire LA

What is P4C?

 Choosing a Stimulus

 Any Questions?

 The Socratic Method ◄

 Facilitating a P4C Enquiry

 Review

 Resources

The Socratic Method

Who was Socrates?

Good P4C facilitation embraces 'The Socratic Method'. The historical Socrates (c.468-399 BC) is something of a mystery to us. He left no written record of his life or teachings, so our knowledge of him is based on accounts of those who knew him, mostly Plato. These reveal a number of features that you should try to emulate with your class:

- Characterisation as an **enquirer**, not as a teacher. Socrates denies the possession of wisdom – at least wisdom in the sense of 'knowing it all'. He asks many questions and offers few firm answers, expecting others to take responsibility for their own thinking and understanding

- An obsession with **definition** (eg of *holiness, courage, beauty*). This derives from his own quest for expert understanding. He would agree that experts know their subject ('subject' here could equally be 'concept') but to him that means understanding what that subject is

- A passion for **ethics** – *how should one live?* – in regard to mundane matters as well as important issues. Far from being a game, or pure 'sophistry,' Socrates' concerns were deadly serious – in his case, literally

- In all the above, a relentless intellectual intensity in the exercise of **reason**

What does this method look like in the classroom?

Good philosophical facilitation is at once very similar to your usual best practice and far removed from it. Consider this compare-and-contrast framework of desirable behaviour:

Classroom discussion	Classroom enquiry
Harmony and concord	Intellectual clashes and reasonable discord (General Patton: *'If everyone's thinking the same, someone isn't thinking.'*)
Maximum participation, evidenced in everyone contributing orally	Maximum engagement, but we're not thinking only when we're talking – sometimes the quieter children are more engaged than the talkative ones (Descartes: *I think, therefore I am.'*)
Working often towards teacher-led objectives	Working consistently towards pupil-led objectives (**IQ** – 'I'm Questioning ....'; **WISE** – 'What I'm Still Exploring ....'; **www**...– 'We Were Wondering ...' **AWOL** – 'Another Way of Looking ...')
Everyone's viewpoint is equally valuable (moral relativism)	Everyone's viewpoint is equally valued, but some may turn out to be more valuable than others (Peter Tatchell: *'All human beings are worthy of respect, but not all ideas are worthy of respect.'*)
A striving for consensus and one shared outcome, resolution or answer	A striving after truth and clarity, but accepting a multiplicity of differing outcomes – each richer and more complex as a result of the shared enquiry (Cardinal John Henry Newman: *'Truth is wrought out by many minds working together freely.'*)

The search for truth

'Truth is not one thing, or even a system. It is an increasing complexity... the knots on the underside of the carpet.' **Adrienne Rich**

A clue to a core principle underpinning your role as a facilitator is glimpsed in the psychologist-philosopher William James' definition of philosophy:

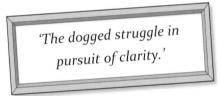

'The dogged struggle in pursuit of clarity.'

It's necessarily tough, and directed towards a viable truth or understanding.

James, like Socrates, was interested in the nature of *truth*. For him, truths are made in the course of human experience and they *'... lead us into useful verbal and conceptual quarters'*. It's your job in the classroom to help construct these truths or clearer understandings in dialogue with others. Socrates provides us with a model for doing this.

Socrates the sensualist

Socrates did for reason what Nigella Lawson would later do for food. Sometimes crudely, frequently with an ironic caress, he would tease, tantalise, flatter, tickle, probe and strip an argument bare in his quest for a viable truth. Intellectual satisfaction – often in the form of definition or commonality – is reached only once there is no further assumption, false premise, or counter-example to explore. And his primary tool? The humble question.

Socrates knew intuitively that the question leads and teases out rather than imposes. In Muriel Spark's classic novel, Miss Jean Brodie knew this too:

> 'To me, education is a leading out of what is already there in the pupil's soul. To Miss Mackay it is a putting in of something that is not there. To me, that is not education, but intrusion.'

This is our model as P4C facilitators – leading out, in the true spirit of *educare*.

Socratic dialogue

The following extract from Socrates' dialogue with Menexenus provides an example of The Socratic Method in action. Through his questions, Socrates makes clear how complex the notion of friendship actually is. Note how he aims to define this concept by continually seeking exceptions:

> Tell me then, when one loves another, is the lover or the beloved the friend? Or may either be the friend?

> Either may, I should think, be the friend of either.

> Do you mean that if only one of them loves the other, they are mutual friends?

> Yes, that is my meaning.

> But what if the lover is not loved in return - which is a very possible case? Or is, perhaps, even hated? Nothing can exceed his love, and yet he imagines either that he is not loved in return, or that he is hated. Is not that true?

> Yes, quite true.

Socratic dialogue

> In that case, the one loves, and the other is loved?

> Yes.

> Then which is the friend of which? Is the lover the friend of the beloved, whether he be loved in return, or hated? Or is the beloved the friend? Or is there no friendship at all on either side, unless they both love one another?

> There would seem to be none at all.

> Then this notion is not in accordance with our previous one. We were saying that both were friends, if one only loved; but now, unless they both love, neither is a friend?

> That appears to be true ....

(No one is nowadays too surprised to learn that Socrates met an early death at the hands of intellectually exhausted Athenians!)

The limits of praise

> 'If we are not accountable [to ourselves], we shall wander the world seeking someone to explain ourselves to, someone to absolve us and tell us we have done well.' **Nietzsche**

Socrates could be rather flattering in his dialogues with others and it may be tempting for you too to seek to reinforce positive contributions, eg: *'Superb philosophy, Ptolemy!', 'Excellent idea, Maria!', 'That connection's really juicy, Lucy!'* Resist the temptation!

Even worse would be to describe individuals – or even the class – as *'outstanding philosophers', 'deep thinkers'*, etc. At least the first examples have the merit of praising a specific action, thought, line of reasoning or disposition – whereas to describe a child or group as a finished product ('deep thinker', etc) is to imply that their job is done, or that someone else's job was less well done, and/or – the most misguided message of all – that the job of your pupils is to impress you and that your job is to reveal when you are impressed.

Praise and motivation

Learning motivation is slaked by the water from two wells:

1 Extrinsic learning motivation relies on an external agent to keep your pupils engaged. External agents include such things as the three Ps: praise, prizes and performance grades. It is the outcomes of the activity that are rewarding so the activity is focused on the *products* of learning.

2 Intrinsic learning motivation refers to that hunger to learn that comes from within your pupils. It is driven by such things as intellectual curiosity, a creative restlessness and a passion truly to master a skill, puzzle or a knowledge domain. The activity itself is satisfying and rewarding. It is focused therefore on the *processes* of learning.

It's important that your pupils learn to engage in an enquiry because it **is intrinsically challenging, rewarding and satisfying** – not a step for the display of erudition or the exposure of ignorance. They need to please or impress no one.

Specific positive feedback

Rather than resorting to quick 'n easy strokes, aim instead to communicate to your enquirers that specific philosophical moves and dispositions are valued. It's not their brilliance, it's their contributing; it's not the product, it's the process:

- *'Can anyone see just how Kareem's **openness/flexibility** has moved our thinking on here?'*
- *'Davina, I'm really struck by the **tenacious/persistent** way you kept plugging away at that idea – say why you think it's important that we understand this idea properly.'*
- *'Jack, you've used a word which could be really helpful to us – what **precisely** do you mean by 'fondness'?*
- *'Has anyone spotted how Abi's shown she's been listening **critically/reflectively** in the enquiry this week?'*
- *'Winston, you seem to have made a **connection** between Maia's thought and Harjit's – could you say a bit more about this link?'*

It's no coincidence that all these examples of specific positive feedback are formative, not summative. Each invites some further response to move the enquiry (and the enquirers) forward.

No praise is better than bad praise

If you don't have the time to offer specific, thoughtful and thought-full feedback, it's best not to offer any praise at all. Carol Dweck, one of the world's foremost researchers in the field of learning motivation, made these comments during her speaking tour of England in 2010:

'Process praise is appreciation and encouragement about what the child is doing, and from that she learns good habits.'

'Good (process) praise requires an investment and for you to understand what the child is saying.'

'No praise is far better than praise that praises something like an innate ability.'

Dialogue vs debate

There's a difference between an authentic philosophical dialogue and a performance-oriented debate. There's a time and a place for both, but not when you're doing P4C:

Philosophical Dialogue	Competitive Debate
Collaborative	Oppositional
Seeks a viable truth or understanding	Seeks victory
It's about learning	It's about performance
Expands one's thinking	Proves or affirms one's thinking
Deals with complexity	Seeks simplicity
Reveals and critiques assumptions	Defends assumptions as truth
To change your mind is OK	To change your mind is to throw in the towel
Shows concern for others – their views, beliefs and feelings	Shows up others – one's own arguments look stronger when theirs look weak
'None of us is as smart as all of us'	*'I am smarter than you'*
Conclusions are tentative	Conclusions are conclusions

The next section looks at the sorts of questions that distinguish a philosophical enquiry from a circle-time discussion, debate, or other good classroom things. Our task is to apply The Socratic Method in the 'marketplace' of a classroom enquiry ....

What is
P4C?

 Choosing a
Stimulus

 Any
Questions?

 The Socratic
Method

 Facilitating a
P4C Enquiry ◄

 Review

 Resources

Facilitating a
P4C Enquiry

Reminder – establish ground rules

So you've arrived at a question for enquiry. Not always one as philosophically rich as those on pages 61-62, but a question nonetheless. **WAIT!** If you haven't already established a few 'rules of engagement' (eg when introducing philosophy or the community of enquiry), try the following script to encourage reflection on the *process* of the enquiry:

> 'Soon we're going to try to answer this question as well as we can, as a whole group. But there are (x) of us in this class. Not everyone's going to get a chance to speak as much as they might wish to speak. Some of us may choose not to speak at all. So what are we all going to have to do to think well together in this enquiry?'

Expect some vague perennials, teacher-pleasers like *'Listen well to each other'*, or *'Be kind [sometimes 'respectful'] to everyone'*. Interrogate these suggestions in more depth: *'How would you know that someone's listening to you?'* (body-language, eye-contact, a comment that builds on your earlier contribution, etc); similarly, 'being kind': *'What does 'being kind' look like?'*, *'Does 'being kind' mean that you shouldn't disagree with someone?'*, etc.

First words

Before committing to the intensity of the enquiry itself, you might want a very brief physical energiser, but in any case call for 30 – 60 secs of silent/private reflection. This will focus everyone on the chosen question and establish a few entry-points for the group enquiry. This is usually followed by a small group dialogue that gives people a chance to release and rehearse their ideas informally before going public, eg:

- **Pair/share** – sharing first thoughts with your neighbour – simple and effective
- **Talking turns** – two lines facing each other and sharing first thoughts with the person opposite for 30 seconds, after which everyone moves one place to the left and repeats the process with a new partner. Three to five encounters should be sufficient
- **Nod or nay** – if the question invites a yes/no response, ask the participants to move around the room *nodding* their heads if they tend to agree, or *folding their arms* if they disagree, then to approach someone who clearly disagrees with them. When pairs have exchanged reasons they move on to new partners. They can change their minds – and required bodily action – at any point in these exchanges
- **Write to reply** – older children could write a sentence or two in response, and be invited to share them in pairs or in public

Enquiry openers

Here are some questions you might use to open up a whole group enquiry:

Question prompt	Possible follow-up	Intention
Are there any important words in this question? (Eg *'Can trees talk?'*)	Underline their choices, ask them to say why they think it's an important word, and choose one to start with: *'So what do we mean by 'talk'?'* Seek examples and counter-examples.	Gets pupils focusing on keyword meanings. Salvages philosophical potential from apparently dead-end or over-complex questions.
Are there any assumptions in this question? (Eg *'Why did Rose pretend she was ill?'*)	Ask for hands/thumbs up if they believe the assumption is a) true, b) untrue, c) partly true and partly untrue. Give reasons.	Reinforces a useful philosophical concept. Encourages deeper meanings and alternative interpretations.

Enquiry openers

Question prompt	Possible follow-up	Intention
Would anyone like to explain what sort of question this is? (Eg *'Do foxes live alone?'*)	Identify the central concept/s in the question ('alone'). Ask how we could squeeze a good enquiry from it. What questions would support this? (Eg *'Why would anyone choose to live alone?'*)	Encourages a meta-questioning stance (getting 'above' the question itself to explore its nature). Alerts pupils to non-enquiry questions (in this instance, quadrant 3 – see page 52) and gets them converting these to enquiry questions.
Who would like to suggest an answer to this question?	Ask for thumbs-up (*'I agree with … because …'*), thumbs-down (*'I disagree with … because …'*) or thumbs-sideways (*'I have a different answer'*).	Launches straight into the question and opens up the dialogue with a range of possibilities. Emphasises reasons and evidence.

Enquiry/community builders

These facilitation 'moves' help participants connect with each other:

Question prompt	Possible follow-up	Intention
Who agrees/disagrees with Emma's point?	Could you say why you agree/disagree?	Establishes levels of support for a position and reasons for it.
Who thinks that Asif really might be on to something here?	What do you like about his point? Why? Could you build on it?	Affirms a pupil's thinking. Encourages close listening to others' contributions. Focuses on key aspects of the contribution.
Could you give us an example from your experience?	Is that a good example? Does anyone have a different experience?	Often 'perks up' the enquiry and helps others connect with it.
How does that fit with what Jo said earlier?	So does your view support Jo's or not? Which view has more evidence? Could you help develop her thought?	Establishes progression. Helps the enquiry connect and cohere. Rescues thoughts raised earlier which risk being forgotten.

Enquiry deepeners

And these 'moves' help participants push their thinking further:

Question prompt	Possible follow-up	Intention
How do you know this?	Does everyone know this? Why? Do only some people know this?	Distinguishing between *a priori* evidence (independent of experience) and *a posteriori* evidence (based on experience).
Is there a general principle? (Eg *'We learn best if we choose what to learn.'*)	Could you explain this principle in more detail? Are there any exceptions?	Pushing for commonalities which link the particular examples. Raising possibility of a deeper truth.
Has anyone got an example to make sense of this?	Does this example help? Do we agree with this? Are there any counter-examples?	Makes the abstract concrete. Exposes an argument for analysis and further exploration.
What is the implication or consequence of this?	Why is this an implication? Whose idea would have a different implication? Does this consequence seem reasonable? Acceptable?	Introduces another 'meta' perspective. Invites inferential thinking. Pursues reasoning to its logical ends.

Enquiry exploders or consolidators

Question prompt	Possible follow-up	Intention
In that case, why don't we just … (… carry on consuming as much as we can? … lie down and die?, etc.)	Any continuation of the devil's advocate role – *'But then we could …'*, *'But you said that …'* etc.	Often acts as a deliberate shock, kick-starting a faltering enquiry. Presents a counter to a prevailing view. Models independent thinking. Confronts implications and consequences.
I have no idea where to go from here. Has anyone got any ideas?	At what point did we seem to get stuck? What are the tricky bits that we need to disentangle? Ah – I see, so if we …?	Models the notion of facilitator as *fallibilistic* co-enquirer. Ensures the participants take responsibility for the enquiry and work as hard as the facilitator. Encourages problem-solving.
Could we try to summarise where we've got to so far?	Could we come up with five important things that we've said?	Consolidates the enquiry prior to Last Words. Encourages meta-thinking.
How much progress have we made with this question?	Are there any important avenues we might have missed so far? Where do we need to go next?	Taking stock and summarising. Getting 'above' the question to get perspective on it.

Dealing with silence

Silence is not ...	Silence is ...	Because ...
A source of embarrassment.	A source of empowerment.	P4C values the power of contributions – not their frequency. Feel the silence; feel the power.
A sign that you've lost your way.	A sign that you're taking the time to find the right way.	Every intervention you make you will affect the course of the enquiry. So don't rush impulsively to action – seek to discern the best available intervention.
An act of omission.	An intentional move.	You are *choosing* to call for silence, or to await a response from the group, or to delay responding to raised hands. You make these choices for a reason.
A base metal.	Golden.	As with gold, in our society silence's value is consequent on its relative rarity. It shimmers in the pan.

Middle Words – be ready to call a 'time out' (or 'middle words') break of 15-30 seconds, or longer, for private thinking or paired conversation whenever you feel it's warranted.

Development – introduce a visual signal (eg hands over ears) that *pupils* can use to call their own time out.

Encouraging meta-questioning

Meta-questioning involves the purposeful questioning of the question itself. Introduce the word 'meta' as meaning *beyond* or *about* and show how it's possible to apply it to many things: questioning, learning, thinking, etc. Use the term frequently and explicitly. It has value at many steps of the P4C process. Examples of use during the enquiry stage:

Facilitation	Intended effect
What exactly is the question asking? Could anyone say just what we need to be examining here?	To focus on the salient elements of the question. To link the words selected to the 'big idea': since words are *'tools, not essences'* (Wittgenstein) the words may only be an approximation to the central idea.
Would anyone like to ask a question about the question?	A full-frontal invitation to meta-questioning that can lead to the exposure of some interesting angles on the question. (NB offer thinking time!)
Does anyone understand this question in a different way from the way we've been following?	To voice and validate the different perspectives of quieter participants, who may otherwise be swept along by the dominant discourse.
Is there anything about the question that we might have missed?	To avoid premature 'closure' and to open some new lines of enquiry.

Judging when to intervene

Nothing captures the essential art of good facilitation better than the decision to intervene – both when and how. It will be necessary to intervene, but there's no hard 'science' or 'praxis' of intervention to fall back on. At different times expect to find yourself positioned at any point on this intervention continuum:

No direct intervention

Frequent, directive intervention

As a rule of thumb, the more experienced the group, the greater the scope for sitting back a bit. This isn't because experienced P4Cers don't need facilitation; rather they can take on more of the facilitation themselves – asking each other for clarifications, evidence, reasons, links, etc. This is the ultimate aim.

Troubleshooting

In the absence of fixed rules, here are a few examples of where facilitative interventions could be triggered:

Trigger	Intervention	Intention
Too many anecdotal contributions.	*'I'm hearing lots of interesting views and stories, but could anyone say how one of these stories might help us to answer our question?'*	To connect the concrete particular (the child's lived experience) to a more general truth – ie to move the enquiry to more conceptual terrain.
Too much abstraction – possibly leaving some people behind.	*'Wow – I'm struggling to get my head around this idea. Could anyone help me with an example – something that could help me understand this?'*	As above, but in reverse. Confirms the facilitator as fallibilistic co-enquirer.
'Scattergun' contributions.	*'Help! I'm finding it difficult to connect all these thoughts. Is there an idea that might link them?'*	To effect greater coherence in the enquiry, so that everyone works together in pursuit of greater clarity.
Repetition of a point already made.	*'Have we already heard Jason's point before? When?'* (To be asked in kindly tones, not sarcastic!)	To encourage close listening and a drive to progression in the enquiry.

Troubleshooting

These 'moves' are intended to address issues around the process of the enquiry:

Trigger	Intervention	Intention
Competitive point-scoring.	*'Remember that we're not trying to beat each other, we're trying to beat the question!'*	To remind everyone that an enquiry isn't a debate – progress is the goal, not victory.
Self-regarding displays of erudition (although there can be value in subject expertise).	*'Sebastian, what is your main point?'* *'Ella, how does that knowledge move us forward in our thinking?'*	To reinforce the search for conceptual clarity, connections and understanding rather than inert knowledge *per se*.
Laughing at (not with) someone's contribution.	*'I'm not sure why some people are laughing – Naz, were you noticing that …?'*	To reinforce respectful consideration of all views. Helps Naz feel that his contribution wasn't so daft after all (but laughing at it was).
Subverting the enquiry (rare).	*'David, could you tell us why you said that?'*	Insisting on personal responsibility for one's contributions.

Supporting struggling enquirers

Most P4C enquiries take place in inclusive classroom contexts, and struggle is a natural element of the process – for everyone. For a variety of reasons individual children might have specific problems with the process. A few techniques to try out:

Difficulty	Before the enquiry	During the enquiry
Attention-needy pupil, fidgety and prone to physical activity.	Consider what specific roles could usefully be played by the pupil to focus attention, eg to track who's doing most of the talking, to produce a mindmap of the enquiry, or to stand at the back of the circle and act as a 'runner' – transferring an object held by the speaker to a new speaker. (This is also a helpful aid to thinking time/reflection, as it takes a few seconds for the runner to get the object to the new speaker.)	• Remind the group about the established ground rules • Use proximal and direct positive feedback (eg for good listening, attentiveness, etc.) whilst consistently ignoring undesirable behaviour • Implement displacement activities (see middle column) • Provide frequent breaks for one-to-one dialogue and short, physical activities

Supporting struggling enquirers

Difficulty	Before the enquiry	During the enquiry
Poor listening skills.	• Have a class discussion about what constitutes good listening and produce a visual prompt sheet of the salient points • Listening games to develop pre-skills (one-to-one)	• Refer to the visual prompt sheet • The child listens out for one or two specific things, eg every time someone says 'I agree/disagree with …' Make a tally of these occurrences and report back at the end
Unpopular child.	• Discreetly pair the child with a popular peer when generating questions • Choose a question-voting system that doesn't expose the child's isolation	• Seek out opportunities to understand and publicly value this child's contributions; make her contributions clear to the community • Sensitively convey that the best thoughts don't necessarily come from celebrities or the best-looking people

Supporting struggling enquirers

Difficulty	Before the enquiry	During the enquiry
Rigid and convergent thinker.	Provide plentiful opportunities for open-ended tasks and activities that are strong on process and underplay one desired solution (eg *'If 12 is the answer, what's the question?'*)	• Emphasise how the best answers need us to explore many answers, including ones that seem nonsensical at first • Notice and reinforce toleration of ambiguity and lack of certainty, and the exploration of multiple options
English as an additional language.	Prime the child with advance experience of the stimulus, and help her to become an 'expert' in it before it's presented to the class.	• Identify and unpack key words • Trust to the P4C process – it grows linguistic expertise

Last words

All enquiries run their course – if only because bells happen. Hold back a few minutes for Last Words, which may be a brief reflective conversation with a partner, or a round as in 'circle time'. This effects a degree of closure on the enquiry and is often when quieter children find their public voice for the first time. Here and over the page are three ways of conducting the round:

1. **Pass a 'conch'** (eg a statuette of *The Thinker* or *'Philosophy Bear'*) around the circle and invite a short final contribution from whoever is holding the object. This could take the form of a summative thought, a new question, something they wish to think more about, or even just one to three words. (The latter can make a sentence or just a list.) NB State the right to 'pass'.

Last words

2. **Write to Reflect** – ask for *brief* last words to be written down on a scrap of paper or sticky note. Anyone may start by reading their words out then placing them in a box or attaching them to a 'knowledge tree' in the centre of the circle, or a display chart. Anyone can follow anyone, but leave a few seconds between each narration, and be sensitive to others wishing to come in.

3. **Show you've changed** (quick 'n easy) – leave your seat and find another if you changed your mind (or thinking) about something during the enquiry.

What is
P4C?

 Choosing a
Stimulus

 Any
Questions?

 The Socratic
Method

 Facilitating a
P4C Enquiry

 Review

 Resources

Review

The importance of reflection

> *'Children don't learn from experience. They learn by reflecting on the experience.'*
> **Neville West**

So, you have facilitated your first few enquiries. Your pupils have responded well to the opportunity for open enquiry and discussion. There is even a sense of growth, both for individuals and for the class. But how can you build on all this?

P4C has always recognised that the key to good learning is **reflection** as well as **enquiry**. Reflection not only clarifies understanding but also consolidates learning – especially learning about learning. You will help the group make the best progress as enquirers if you encourage them to reflect *together* on the very process of enquiry – to think about the manner of their thinking as well as its content. Try to create time for formal **Review** – ideally at the end of the session or the day, or perhaps at the end of the week.

Reviewing content – visual representations

'Let's do some meta-learning' as a way in to deep reflection will probably be asking too much of your pupils! A better first step might be to ask them to review the 'content' of the enquiry, but *as a whole*.

A visual representation of an enquiry such as a flowmap or mindmap (organised conceptually, rather than chronologically) can be particularly helpful in highlighting the major shifts in your pupils' thinking. Talking about these shifts would enable them to see that good thinking consists of being ready to make such strategic moves as:

- Questioning assumptions or claims
- Providing examples or counter-examples
- Connecting or comparing concepts
- Drawing distinctions

Reviewing content – other ideas

The simplest way of constructing flowmaps or mindmaps is to focus on key words or concepts. These could be drawn from Last Words – either as they proceed, or from a group 'thought shower' at the end. But here are some other possibilities:

- Invite 'trackers' or **'big theme hunters'** to track the enquiry as it proceeds – on a flipchart if they are willing, or in their personal thoughtbooks as an aide memoire for later Review. You might encourage noting of the thinker as well as the thought

- Put the focus on questions rather than concepts. Invite **'question monitors'** to listen for new questions during an enquiry and make sure that they are recorded. Explore the connections between these questions and the original(s) to aid strategic thinking

- Focus on **'thinking vocabulary'** (or what one P4Cer calls 'little concepts for big thinking'), eg fact/opinion, agree/disagree, evidence/reason. Encourage your class to build its own list of such words and to note whenever they come up during enquiry

- **Video-record** the enquiry, with good ideas or thinking highlighted on (re)viewing

Some basic evaluation tools

Reviewing is not done merely to recollect the thinking that has gone on, but to evaluate it. It should be guided by the question, *'What can we learn from this enquiry that would help us to do it better next time?'* There is a range of basic tools or frameworks to help with this.

The simplest is de Bono's **PMI** (or, **P**lus/positive, **M**inus/negative and **I**nteresting/neutral).

The PMI can be used to evaluate any aspect of the enquiry, but it is particularly useful in regard to the various stages. Small groups or the whole class could be asked to evaluate the starter activity, or the stimulus, or the question-choosing, etc.

Other favourite 'tools' are:
*   **www.ebi** (**w**hat **w**ent **w**ell, **e**ven **b**etter **i**f)
*   **'A star and a wish'**
    (something that went well, and a
    suggestion for improvement)

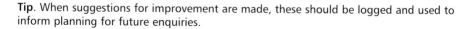

Tip. When suggestions for improvement are made, these should be logged and used to inform planning for future enquiries.

Checking the basic conventions

Another simple focus for Review can be the basic conventions outlined in the first chapter of this Pocketbook. These can be especially valuable in the early days of forming a community of enquiry. To add depth to the evaluation you might review these not just as one-off behaviours but as habits or virtues whose growth could be observed over time.

For example, the community could be asked to consider how well they succeeded in being:

S erious – respecting others and their ideas (so, not interrupting – OOPSAAT)

O pen-minded – being flexible, ie ready to change your mind

C onstructive – deliberately working towards better ideas and behaviours

R easonable – giving and accepting reasons, and drawing conclusions

A miable – being friendly, disagreeing without being disagreeable

T enacious – thinking things through, and standing bravely by your beliefs

E mpathetic – appreciating others' feelings and experiences

S unny – showing a sense of humour and optimism

Tip. Explaining and exemplifying these virtues in other ways would be part of the Review, as would encouraging the adoption and development of new conventions and virtues.

The 4C framework

We referred earlier in the book to 4C Thinking. This can be regarded as the major framework for more advanced evaluation of communities of enquiry. Here it is again, in tabular form:

Mode of thinking	Most obvious practices	Simple explanation
Caring	Listening and Valuing	Thinking of others
Collaborative	Speaking and Supporting	Thinking with others
Creative	Suggesting and Connecting	Thinking for yourself
Critical	Questioning and Reasoning	Thinking about thinking

You could see each of these modes of thinking as operating independently, or even in contrary directions (eg creative vs critical, or critical vs caring). But in P4C they are seen as complementary, and a deliberate attempt is made to develop them in harmony. The community of enquiry is a group of **critical friends**, trying to create better ideas together.

Caring thinking – what to look for (basic)

Matthew Lipman invented the notion of 'caring' thinking to counter a tendency towards over-emphasis on critical thinking. His notion of the caring thinker was of one who was sensitive to other people, perspectives and purposes – a **reasonable**, not merely reasoning, person. And a basic mark of such a person is that they are as good at listening as they are at speaking (or even better!).

It is possible, of course, to 'test' whether someone has been listening by asking them to repeat what has been said, but this is too 'teacherly' a strategy for use in P4C. A better process is to stop an enquiry occasionally and ask people in pairs to remind each other of what X has just said – or, more ambitiously, what the last three speakers said.

In Review, you could ask pairs to talk with each other about whether they think people are getting better at listening, and if so what **evidence** there is for that.

Tip. Encourage them to list different forms of evidence (such as 'not interrupting') on a 'Caring Thinking' chart – and encourage reference to this chart in all lessons, not just P4C.

Caring thinking – what to look for (advanced)

More advanced evidence for good listening that might appear on the chart could be:
- Responses directed to previous speakers, using their names
- Related remarks, ie ones that are explicitly connected to previous points

Tip. Such behaviours are easy enough to note during a session or in Review, but a most effective way of highlighting them would be to video an enquiry and review it soon after.

Caring thinking can be evaluated at an even deeper level. Ann Sharp, Lipman's closest associate, explained it as **appreciative thinking**, ie not merely recognising that others had different perspectives and purposes, but valuing what they had to offer. Try asking anyone to 'celebrate' something that someone else said that they particularly liked. Avoid celebrating particular ideas yourself – it could undermine pupils' confidence in their own judgement – but be ready to celebrate instances of **care in communication**, ie *how* pupils express themselves.

This could be set as a focus for a session – but make sure then that it is also a focus for evaluation in the Review.

Collaborative thinking – what to look for (basic)

Of the 4Cs, collaborative thinking is perhaps the most difficult to pin down in words but the most pervasive in a healthy community of enquiry. The very notion of 'community' implies that people are working together. But how does this become a mode of thinking, and how is it evidenced and evaluated?

As a mode of thinking it is very much the opposite of 'competitive' thinking, such as may be encouraged by debate. It is thinking conditioned by the desire to be of constructive help to others. Here are ways in which it could be evidenced, evaluated and encouraged:

- Playing a positive part in activities, including question-making and voting
- Being ready to speak and contribute to the enquiry
- Being supportive of others who are trying to speak or express themselves
- Employing encouraging body language (smiling, nodding, etc.)

Collaborative thinking – what to look for (advanced)

As a community of enquiry becomes more mature – perhaps after half a year of regular enquiry – you might expect to see all sorts of changes in the attitudes of the members. Your pupils will be less fussy about who they work and talk with. They will be generally more helpful (not only in philosophical enquiries). This might be a mark of more caring thinking too.

It is harder to mark the progress in attitudes than in skills. However, notice any evidence of readiness to put the interests of others ahead of one's own, eg:

*   If a child 'gives way' for another to speak first
*   If someone consciously acts as a mediator between two points of view
*   If people volunteer more readily

One of the most satisfying marks of collaborative thinking is when children begin to take **responsibility for the process** of enquiry itself, eg by suggesting stimuli, or leading different steps, such as question-airing or voting, or even the enquiry itself. Hand over such responsibility whenever you can.

Creative thinking – what to look for (basic)

> *'Creativity is the power to connect the seemingly unconnected.'*
> **William Plomer, (1903-1973)**

P4C focuses on creating *ideas*, rather than *products*. Creative ideas often get expressed during enquiries. Almost every verbal contribution to an enquiry can be regarded as a unique product of the moment. Sometimes speakers even surprise themselves by what they say!

Tip. Try to put names to creative moves when you hear them, eg:

- 'Thank you for that **suggestion**'
- 'That sounds like an **alternative**'
- 'That's a good **connection**'

This makes it easier to identify the moves in Review, and also encourages pupils to practise such moves in future.

Creative thinking – what to look for (advanced)

> '[Man's] mind, once stretched by a new idea, never regains its original dimensions'
> **Oliver Wendell Holmes**

Philosophical enquiry aims to **make sense**. As a form of making, sense-making is a creative process in itself. Even at the level of 'knowing facts', there is some sense-making to be done. At the level of interpreting people's emotions and values an enormous amount of creativity is required – partly through imagination and empathy. This is the steady task of philosophical enquiry: both you and your pupils should be aware that you are actively constructing new meanings for each other.

Tip. If you find it hard to make sense of what is said, don't hesitate to ask for **clarification**. When your pupils follow your model and check each other's meanings (or even your own!) you will know that they are becoming active sense-makers.

A good metaphor for creative thinking is that of 'stretching' the mind to think in new ways. Pairs could be asked in Review to discuss how their thinking (and feeling) has been stretched (ie challenged and enlarged) during the enquiry.

Critical thinking – what to look for (basic)

The root meaning of the word 'critical' is 'judgement', and of course this includes positive as well as negative evaluation and decision-making. In P4C your pupils are encouraged to think about thinking – their classmates' and their own – and to make their own best judgements in response. In essence, they are deciding which ideas to believe or value or even to live by.

Questioning and reasoning are closely tied in with such thinking. Questioning provides the impetus towards better thinking, and reasoning provides us with a framework within which to develop and evaluate ideas.

Tip. Questions of all sorts should be encouraged and evaluated, either as they come up, or during Review. Similarly, 'moves' in argument should be noted, ideally as they take place. Here are key words to model, and to monitor in their take-up:

but, so, if, then, because, either, or, might, would, not, always, never, same, different

argument, valid, premise, evidence, reason, implies, follows, conclusion, compare

Critical thinking – what to look for (advanced)

We can be more specific about the sorts of questions and language of argumentation that you should aim for in an advanced community of enquiry.

Questions may be asked for the following precise purposes. To:

- **Clarify** – if the meaning is not clear
- **Exemplify** – if an example would make the meaning more vivid
- **Simplify** – if much has been said and there is a need for 'the essence'
- **Amplify** – if not enough has been said, and more detail is needed
- **Testify** – if some first-hand experience would help persuade
- **Justify** – if some support is needed for a belief
- **Quantify** – if the extent of a claim needs to be checked
- **Qualify** – if an exception or distinction needs to be drawn

Tip. Print and distribute the words above for every pupil and invite them to try to use their word during an enquiry. This will provide a critical thinking focus – but make sure to evaluate and consolidate the skills in Review. (By all means use synonyms such as 'elaborate' for 'amplify', 'witness' for 'testify'; 'check' or 'gauge' for 'quantify'.)

From reflection to resolution

A Review can look back on a variety of thinking skills. But there is more to being a good thinker than just outward skills, and P4C places particular value on developing **dispositions**. In P4C, Reviews are seen as part of a larger enterprise in which your pupils help each other to construct not only common understandings and community behaviours, but also personal qualities and characters.

So, your qualities as a philosophical teacher – intellectual humility, breadth of mind, respect and reasonableness – might equally be encouraged in your pupils and be evaluated in their own right. So might the qualities signalled by the SOCRATES acronym on page 98.

And whatever list of personal qualities or strengths you are guided by, among the most important is 'resolution' – the determination, on reflection, to do better in future. Reviews should always end positively with '*So, what next?*'

Planning

As well as evaluating and planning for skills and disposition development, you could profitably spend some part of the Review looking again at the content of the enquiry and connecting it with other areas of enquiry and curriculum.

Tip. During Review, ask if there were any ideas/concepts from the stimulus or the enquiry that anyone would like to follow up. Perhaps you could offer to provide an exercise or discussion plan to extend their thinking. Or you could suggest some area of the curriculum that could be explored with the concepts in mind.

It could become quite normal to ask the practical question, *'Does anyone have any ideas about what we might use as a stimulus for the next enquiry?'*

The suggestions that pupils come up with – such as advertisements, songs, video clips – might tell you a lot about how they are able to connect and construct their own learning.

Inherent as well as instrumental value

After all this attention to the skills and habits that philosophical enquiry can develop, let's not forget that it can be enjoyed as a **good in itself**. It is fine to look for signs of progress and room for improvement, but we should not become obsessed with detail and measurement. P4C is not only of value if it leads instrumentally to better results in something else. We jump through enough classroom hoops as it is!

Feel free to celebrate a 'good' enquiry without feeling the need for measurement. Enquiries can reach parts that other lessons don't. You'll be able to tell just from the engagement of the participants or from remarks such as *'My brain hurts'*.

Gauges of success can be as simple as showing 'thumbs up' at the end or encouraging young people to share their enthusiasm and ideas with parents that evening.

Securing P4C in the curriculum

P4C often has an immediate positive impact on both learners and teachers, freeing them up to explore new ideas in new ways. But it does require risk-taking and commitment from you and your school, and the impact can fade if P4C is not regularly timetabled.

Each school is different and each school will be able to find its own creative solution to embedding P4C in the curriculum. The next page offers some suggestions.

Gold, silver and bronze routes to embedding P4C

	Bronze	Silver	Gold
	1 hour a week	**1.5 hours a week**	**2 hours per week**
How?	Speaking/listening or Literacy lesson.	Speaking/listening or Literacy lesson at start of the week + half an hour at end of each week for Review and Planning.	Speaking/listening or Literacy + two further half hours – one for Review and Planning; one for 'Rehearsal', ie practice of particular skills.
Review	Every 4th session – part of APP AfL skills: 1. Social/communicative. 2. Emotional/affective. 3. Thinking/cognitive. 4. Personal/interests/values. Also making links with other learning in curriculum, eg Maths, History, Science.	Focuses as for bronze, but more detail; planning further questions/stimuli for **reflection** (for next session) and further questions for **research** (in other parts of the curriculum). Also, possible to link more systematically with SEAL and/or PSHE.	As for silver, but the additional 'Rehearsal' session would focus on an agreed skill/disposition, using exercises drawn from a bank, eg www.p4c.com, or developed by you.

What is
P4C?

 Choosing a
Stimulus

 Any
Questions?

 The Socratic
Method

 Facilitating a
P4C Enquiry

 Review

 Resources

Resources

Training

So you've got this far. Thank you. If you haven't already tried out P4C our guess is that you're one of the following:

a) Insanely excited and wanting to put it into practice immediately.

b) Reserving judgment and wanting to find out more.

c) Bored witless but have OCD tendencies – so you'll read on to the bitter end before consigning this Pocketbook to your impeccably alphabetised collection.

Might we assume a) or b)? If so, the best resource you could possibly access to support your experimentation or further exploration is high-quality training in P4C. Whilst we have worked tirelessly (OK, intermittently) to make this Pocketbook as helpful as possible, nothing is as helpful in gaining a grasp of an experiential process as actually experiencing that process. Since 1990, the educational charity SAPERE (www.sapere.org.uk) has been offering and delivering accredited, hands-on training in P4C. Please help it to continue doing so. Remember, *'Hands-on doesn't mean brains-off'* **(Joe Renzulli).**

Other useful websites

http://www.icpic.org/ (Worldwide P4C network)

http://cehs.montclair.edu/academic/iapc/ (Institute for the Advancement of Philosophy for Children, New Jersey – original site of P4C)

http://p4c.org.nz/Home.php (among the clearest of several international sites)

http://www.teachingchildrenphilosophy.org/wiki/Main_Page (USA site with excellent advice and resources)

http://depts.washington.edu/nwcenter/index.html (site of the Northwest Center in Seattle, USA, including 'Wondering Aloud' – a practical blog from the director)

http://www.hent.org/hent/hentnews/philo_children_class.htm (a report on classroom practice from the Holistic Education Network, Tasmania)

http://menon.eu.org/ (an ambitious P4C project involving 11 European countries)

http://www.tandfonline.com/doi/abs/10.1080/0267152042000248016

Recommended background reading

Ideally in conjunction with high-quality training, the following titles all offer something to your developing expertise:

Children as Philosophers – Learning Through Enquiry and Dialogue in the Primary Classroom
by Joanna Haynes. Published by Routledge, 2008 (steeped in P4C practice, and doesn't shirk the niggly issues that arise)

Critical Thinking in Young Minds
by Victor Quinn. Published by David Fulton, 1997 (not P4C *per se*, but the best possible monument to a critical thinking middle-aged mind who died in his prime)

Philosophy in the Classroom
by Matthew Lipman et al. Published by Temple University Press, 1980 (over three decades old, but far from dated – still an excellent introduction to P4C)

Little Big Minds – Sharing Philosophy with Kids
by Marietta McCarty. Published by Tarcher/Penguin, 2006 (again, not P4C *per se*, but a super resource which does what it says on the tin)

Recommended background reading

Philosophy with Teenagers –
nurturing a moral imagination
for the 21st century
by Patricia Hannam & Eugenio
Echeverria. Published by Network
Continuum, 2009 (the title itself
offers a great response to any
OfSTED query about your practice:
'Well, I'm in the process of
developing a moral imagination for
the 21st century – is that OK?')

Teaching Thinking
by Robert Fisher. Published by
Continuum, 2003 (a superb
introduction to the Socratic
approach to education) or
Creative Dialogue Routledge,
2009

The School and Society and *The Child*
and the Curriculum
by John Dewey. Published by University of
Chicago Press, 1990 (seminal works from one of
P4C's granddaddies) or check out *My Pedagogic*
Creed on http://dewey.pragmatism.org/creed.htm

The Story of Philosophy
by Brian Magee. Published by Dorling Kindersley,
1998 (a masterfully accessible and succinct
introduction to the sweep of western philosophy)

Thinking in Education
by Matthew Lipman. Published by Cambridge
University Press, 2003 (a core text written by the
man himself)

Thinking Together – Philosophical Enquiry
for the Classroom
by Philip Cam. Published by Hale & Iremonger,
1995

Classroom-ready resources

F/KS1 – ages 3-7

But Why? Developing Philosophical Thinking in the Classroom (teacher's manual)
by Sara Stanley with Steve Bowkett. Published by Network Educational Press, 2004

First Stories for Thinking and First Poems for Thinking
by Robert Fisher. Published by Nash Pollock, 1999 and 2000

Helping Young Children to Ask Questions
by Vicky Charlesworth. Published by Lawrence Educational, 2004

Philosophy for Children – Ideas and activities to unlock current topics
by Marilyn Bowles (part of the Key Issues series). Published by A C Black, 2008

Storywise
by Karen Murris & J Haynes. Published by Dialogue works, 2000
(an excellent manual to support eight classic picture books; also available as an e-book
through www.p4c.com)

Classroom-ready resources

KS2-3 – ages 7-14

20 Thinking Tools by Philip Cam. Published by ACER Press, 2006
Games/Stories/Poems/Values for Thinking by Robert Fisher. Published by Nash Pollock, 1996-2001
Philosophy Through Storytelling by Pauline Purcell. Published by Speechmark, 2010
Philosophy in the Classroom by Ron Shaw. Published by Routledge, 2008
Thinking Stories 1-3, plus *Teacher Resource/Activity Books*, Philip Cam (ed.). Published by Hale & Iremonger, 1993, 1994,1997

KS3-5 – ages 14-18

Socratic Circles – fostering critical and creative thinking in middle and high school by Matt Copeland. Published by Stenhouse Publishers, 2005
The Philosophy Files (1&2) by Stephen Law. Published by Orion Children's Books, 2000, 2003
The Pig That Wants to be Eaten – and 99 other thought experiments by Julian Baggini. Published by Granta Books, 2005
The Simpsons and Philosophy – the D'oh! Of Homer by William Irwin et al. Published by Carus Publishing, 2001
Newswise by R. Sutcliffe & S. Williams (News articles of perennial interest, published on CD by www.dialogueworks.co.uk, or available individually, among many other resources, on www.p4c.com, the online resource/collaboration service)

Cracking picture books (F/KS1 – ages 3-7)

Author	Title	Theme
Jez Alborough	Some Dogs Do	Self-belief/aiming high
Peter Bowman	I Wish I Were Big	Aspirations/contentment
John Burningham	Would you rather …	Choices
John Bush & Korky Paul	The Fish Who Could Wish	Greed/wisdom
Eric Carle	The Bad-Tempered Ladybird	Picking a fight/sharing
Eric Carle	The Very Hungry Caterpillar	Change/Growth/Food
Julia Donaldson & Axel Scheffler	The Gruffalo	Mind over matter
Mem Fox & Vladimir Radunsky	Where the Giant Sleeps	Dreams/mythic creatures
Helme Heine	The Most Wonderful Egg in the World	Beauty/perfection
Pat Hutchins	The Very Worst Monster	Being ignored in the family
Pat Hutchins	Clocks and More Clocks	Nature of time
Maurice Sendak	Where the Wild Things Are	Wild/tame

Cracking picture books (KS2 – ages 7-11)

Author	Title	Theme
Istvan Banyai	Zoom	Looking closer, deeper, further
Anthony Browne	Piggybook	Sexism
Michael Foreman	A Child's Garden – A story of hope	Hope/reconciliation
Toby Forward & Izhar Cohen	The Wolf's Story	Contrasting perspectives
Roberto Innocenti & Ian McEwan	Rose Blanche	A child's experience of war
Colin McNaughton & Satoshi Kitamura	Once Upon an Ordinary School Day	Imagination/thinking the impossible
Hiawyn Oram & Satoshi Kitamura	In the Attic	Perception/possibilities/imagination
Jon Scieszka & Lane Smith	Squids Will Be Squids	Fables for our time
Dyan Sheldon & Gary Blythe	The Garden	Links with the past/stewardship
Shaun Tan	The Red Tree	Hope/coping with adversities
Colin Thompson	Falling Angels	Dreams/possibilities/death
Chris Van Allsburg	The Stranger	Seasons/change/acceptance

Cracking picture books (KS3/4 – ages 11-16)

Author	Title	Theme
Neil Gaiman & Dave McKean	The Day I Swapped my Dad for Two Goldfish	Family life/sibling rivalry
John Marsden & Shaun Tan	The Rabbits	Historical 'voice'/immigration
Jon Scieszka & Lane Smith	The Stinky Cheese Man and Other Fairly Stupid Tales	Anarchic, postmodernist retellings of familiar stories
Jon Scieszka & Lane Smith	Squids Will Be Squids	Fables for our time
Shel Silverstein	The Giving Tree	Giving/love
Shaun Tan	The Red Tree	Hope/coping with adversities
Shaun Tan	The Lost Thing	Belonging/fitting in
Shaun Tan	The Arrival	Immigration (long, wordless picturebook)
Colin Thompson	The Tower to the Sun	The environment/stewardship
Colin Thompson	Falling Angels	Dreams/possibilities/death
Colin Thompson	How to Live Forever	Wisdom/search for meaning
Margaret Wild & Ron Brooks	Fox	Betrayal/deceit/friendship/ambition

Change places if ... (procedure)

We recommend that you sometimes engineer opportunities for your pupils to work with peers that they might not normally gravitate to (see page 24). Here are a few more ways of achieving this:

Participants should be seated as close to a circle as possible, with no obstacles (such as books or bags) within the circle. The facilitator says, *'Change places if ...'*, followed by a statement that might apply to some but not all of the circle. (For a sample range, see below.) Those to whom the statement applies change places, and after a few rounds the group will be well and truly mixed.

This activity can be repeated on different occasions, introducing new challenge and vocabulary. For example, the first time you might concentrate on children's **experiences** – explained as 'things' that have happened to you. The second time you might help the children investigate the idea of **properties** – explained as things that belong to them. Other areas of exploration could be **achievements**, **abilities**, **knowledge**, **preferences**, **opinions**, etc.

Change places if … (examples)

Sample sentences for 'Change Places If …'

1. Change places if you have been … pushed underwater

2. Change places if you have … a pair of flip-flops

3. Change places if you have … climbed to the top of a tree

4. Change places if you can … read upside down

5. Change places if you know … who is the Prime Minister of the UK

6. Change places if you prefer … orange to apple juice

7. Change places if you think that … school should start and end earlier

8. Change places if you … have a younger brother

9. Change places if you … enjoy art/maths/PE etc

10. Change places if you … haven't already changed places

Quotations

If you have wall space that can be given over to thinking and/or P4C, you might wish to display a few useful quotations to provoke reflection. Change them from time to time. Invite pupils to reflect on them, and to share their thoughts with others. Ask them to look out for quotations that appeal to them and bring them in. Don't underestimate their ability to engage with apparently 'over-complicated' quotations – they might enjoy the struggle!

'Most people are other people. Their thoughts are someone else's opinion, their lives a mimicry, their passions – a quotation.' **Oscar Wilde**

'The aim of argument or of discussion should not be victory, but progress.' **Joseph Joubert**

'No problem can withstand the assault of sustained thinking.' **Voltaire**

'Though people can think for themselves, they cannot think by themselves.' **Lawrence Stenhouse**

'He who travels fast travels alone. He who travels far, travels in the company of others.' **African proverb**

'The sleep of reason breeds monsters.' **Goya**

'Improvement makes straight roads, but the crooked roads without improvement are roads of genius.' **William Blake**

Quotations

'Everything in some way connects to everything else.' (**Leonardo da Vinci**)

'Talent for perceiving analogies is the leading fact in genius of every order.'
William James

'It is important that pupils bring a certain ragamuffin, barefoot irreverence to their studies. They are not here to worship what is known, but to question it.'
Jacob Bronowski

'The unexamined life is not worth living.'
Socrates

'You cannot teach a man anything. You can only help him discover it within himself.'
Galileo

'If a teacher is indeed wise, he does not bid you enter the house of his wisdom, but rather leads you to the threshold of your own mind.'
Kahlil Gibran

'There is more to be learned from the unexpected questions of children than the discourses of men.'
John Locke

'A prudent question is one half of wisdom.' **Francis Bacon**

'It is not the answer that enlightens, but the question.' **Eugene Ionesco**

'I not only use all the brains I have, but all that I can borrow.'
Woodrow Wilson

Some concluding words

We hope very much that you have enjoyed browsing our P4C Pocketbook, and that it inspires you to get philosophising with your class. We have no doubt, from our own experiences, that both you and your pupils will profit greatly from regular engagement in this process. Every enquiry we have the pleasure of facilitating reminds us of P4C's joys and its challenges in equal measure.

We leave the last words to a teacher and a pupil from two schools in Southwark, a Local Authority where P4C is well-embedded:

'Philosophy makes the shy people brave and the brave people braver.'
Y4 pupil

'I thought that P4C was just another namby pamby thing being introduced, but I just can't believe the difference it has made to my class – not just in their work but in their attitude to each other.' **Y6 teacher**

About the authors

Barry Hymer

Barry is the Osiris professor of psychology in education at the University of Cumbria. He taught in the primary and secondary sectors before training and practising as an educational psychologist and then founding an education consultancy. He is the author or editor of seven books and numerous papers in the fields of gifted education and thinking skills, including the bestselling, radical and influential Gifted & Talented Pocketbook. In 2003 Barry received the biennial Award for Excellence in Interpreting Philosophy with Children from ICPIC, the International Council for Philosophical Inquiry with Children.

Roger Sutcliffe

Roger read Philosophy at Oxford, then taught in a junior school before joining the Maths department at Christ's Hospital School, Horsham. In the early 90s he trained in Philosophy for Children with Matthew Lipman and has been a freelance trainer ever since. Roger was a founder member of SAPERE and became President in 2003, when he was also elected President of ICPIC. He is the author of *The Philosophy Club*, and of *Newswise*, a current affairs resource. He was co-designer of the International GCSE 'Global Perspectives', and is co-director of p4c.com, the online resource and collaboration service for p4c worldwide. He is also a consultant with www.thinkingschool.co.uk.